Swimming Swimmers Swimming

Swimming Swimmers Swimming

poems

Percival Everett

 RED HEN PRESS | Pasadena, California

Swimming Swimmers Swimming
Copyright © 2011 by Percival Everett

Book design by Mark E. Cull
Book layout by Kathrine Davidson

Library of Congress information:
Everett, Percival L.
Swimming swimmers swimming / Percival Everett.
p. cm.
Includes bibliographical references and index.
ISBN 978-1-59709-478-8 (pbk.)
I. Title.
PS3555.V34S95 2011
811.'54—dc22
2010046971

The California Arts Council, the Los Angeles County Arts Commission, the National Endowment for the Arts, and Los Angeles Department of Cultural Affairs partially support Red Hen Press.

Published by Red Hen Press
www.redhen.org
First Edition

For Anne-Laure Tissut

TABLE OF CONTENTS

Swimming Swimmers Swimming

WEEDY WEEDS

we're not talking about the same place
the place I know is still there still

untouched still still with the wind
moving through the trees and the tree

dogs sniffing at the banks of the stream
sniff dogs sniff at the weedy banks

and we're not talking the same about
some place someplace same place

that I once knew and you know but
I knew the stream with decent flow

the banks with decent trees coverage
shelter for the swimming swimmers

swimming in the swimming pools
where the dogs sniff along the weedy

shore lined with roots and weeds all
weedy and rooted and we're not

talking about the same place someplace
lost amongst the reeds and the weeds

standing wet as moose hair and slick
as trout skin and high as a swallow

swoops through the dusk in the dusky dusk
and bats flap through the batty night

wolves wolving their yowly howls
while in the weedy weeds we hide.

INSINUATION

1

And it starts with a conjunction,
When the night sprawls beneath itself
Like a dream beneath a thought;
I believe it starts in hollow canyons,
Echoes and whispers
Of endless songs and evenings,
swinging doors on terraces:
Trails that track like insistent memories
Of concealed and alluring mark,
To trouble you with an irresistible question—

In rooms where artists sleep,
The forge shows no sign of wear.

2

The beige smog that combs the cilia
of our lungs,
The beige days that brush the blue of
night aside,
Hovering over desert breezes that do not move,
Settles its beige sides beside us in cars,
And into our beds where on cool nights,
We fold like babies into sleep.

Like some coy mistress
The beige smoke rides like a passenger,
Touching elbows with us;
Oh, coy mistress, there will be time
To ready for that which requires readiness;
Coy mistress, take life and make it,
All the work of your smoke hands
That pause and begin your logic;
Coy mistress for us all,
And yet for none of us, a hundred rejections,
A hundred rewritings and revisits
Before we sit and have coffee.

3

In rooms where artists sleep,
The forge shows no sign of wear.
And yes coy mistress, to ask,
Where is the sense? Why are we lost?
Curl back into the sky, while
I gray at my temples—
(Children do not lie about age)
And I shiver in the desert morning cool,
In shirtsleeves but enough—
The shivering is sweet memory.
I will call out into the last of night
And change my mind about so much.

4

The knowledge is persistent,
The premises questionable—
Sun following moon following sun
Until the moon catches up;
Straining against mockingbird,
That strain again!

The voice is one I know, all the voices—
That find familiar timbre and phrase,
And when they dissect me on that table,
How will I appear?
That strain again!

The voice is one I know, all the voices—
Some relic, done with and cast aside
(But here in this din, a song)
Is it sweet breath
That pauses me?
High notes that stretch like promises
across the room.
That strain again!

5

And have I wandered those steep
canyons,
listened to the songs rising from
throats
Of lost people, kneeling in mud, red
and slick?

I should have been a hawk's eyes
Raking the ground below me.

6

The sun finds an west-facing wall,
sweetly!
Stretched by the sky into ribbons,
Dead before it sets, tired,
Prone on the red dirt between us.
Should I, after we share this apple,
Have reason enough amid
this confusion?
But though I shade my eyes,
know the sun will return from the
dead.
Dives off a high place above the
river,
My posture and moment of greatness,
this I saw.
Afraid, I saw it.

7

Around that fire, that circle,
It would have all been worth the
hike,
Among the sage and junipers,
To have chopped off with the turn
of my head,
To have rolled the canyon and the mountains
Into a hand.
Ask any zombie, maybe even Lazarus
himself,
And he will tell you,
Returning from the dead is not
The same as being alive.

8

And would that morning
Be as sweet as the night's rain?
After the owls have settled,
The coyotes singing ceased,
Kissing new shadows to the roots
of trees?
But none of this is what I see.

9

Crippled by indecisiveness,
Will I ever pass by that wind with purpose?
Pragmatic and lost in a sea of doubt,
Will obscuring meaning be enough
To find me to the river's edge?
I will not hear the birds there
Because of the roar of the water,
As if they would sing to me anyway, in this
place.

It will be a child's voice
That leads me brow deep into the flow.

AVERAGES

these words mean
mean words
mean words
cover what can
be covered
setting the stage
in stages
staged by some
stagy stage
ridden from
ridden through
riddled through
and through
and thoroughly
riddled with words
mean words
mean words
these words mean
what they mean
how they mean how mean
theses words
mean

OF SEEING

The lovers' glance, the lover's glance,
the seen is also the victim, also the prisoner,
held in the unwavering gaze, *le regard, le regard,*
a cruel dialectic, a benign reciprocity.

Unlike my words, my sight gives only the present,
cannot perceive past or future, but alleges
spatiality, would have me believe in the
spaces between the things I call things.

No, no, I say, these issues are
normative as well as cognitive, these issues,
divinely construed congruence notwithstanding.
The vanishing point is never the same

for me ever, my never occupying the
same point in space, only, maybe the same
point in time. But words give me that. Sight
is decorporealized and transcendental.

Reports of what was seen
mean little or nothing without what was seen,
there being no standard for veracity without what was seen,
only appeals to words representing the act

of seeing.

Always

never never

never never

never

never

never believe

that never

never never

come

to never

never be

be never

never never

never never

never

never

CRUELTY

there is no sentence
as cruel as the one applied
by a judge to a subject

with no object but infinite verb
forever running on looking
lacking liking licking

parole, some play
some yard, infinite verb
judge to be judged to

be locked by period
by narks against against
as cruel as the one applied

because a cause caused
because adding, adding
adder added.

GRAMMAR

and she cries.
and he cries.
cries and he.
and cries she.
he and cries.
.cries she and

1, 2, 3 . . .

Ask a little question.
Beg hard against a lie.
Count as high as you can.
How many knees can you put on the ground?

Raise a forehead.
Lock a mission.
Count as high as you can?
How many storms will blow up your skirt?

Push a small wagon.
List to another aside.
Count as high as you can.
How many paper hats make a head?

Libellule

being the *fort* of a *da*
and the *da* of a *fort*
qua
qua
despite the appeal.
let the head
fall off the shoulders
into sleep,
Choang-tsu notwithstanding.
the split
after awakening
persists
brings fire
when it falls.
whatever is repetition,
is varied,
modulated,
is merely
alienation of
some meaning.
da da da
fort

FOVEA

a true story
of course a true story
young
intellectual
desperate.
involves a small boat,
a few people,
a small port.
a frail craft,
risk
of course risk,
distancing,
nets,
waves,
a dead gull
floating, tangled.
see him? See him?
he said.
well, he doesn't
see you,
he said,
he doesn't see you.

·

Bones

for Henry

dining on a dinosaur,
he dines with dimes and doughnuts,
deigning to dine when done
with the dinosaur deal,
diddly, diddly, diddly,
the dinosaur dance.

The Unseen

for Joseph Dane

the concealing
being as a whole
proper untruth.
older than
letting-be itself,
disclosing, holding
the concealed.
comport the self itself
toward concealing.
die Verbergung.
des Verborgenen.
being as a whole
as such attunes
and accords,
accordingly,
ceaselessly,
older than letting-be.
definite, determined,
older than blood
letting be blood,
the mystery of
concealing the concealed
letting of the be
letting-be, perhaps.
Vielleicht ist eine halbe
Lüge.

Rows

for Fanny

the rose
and the book
are the same
color.
the book
and the rose
are the same color.
the book
is open
like a rose
has leaves
like a book
has color
like the rose
has meaning
like the color
has thorns
like the book
has thorns
like the meaning
has thorns
like the rose
is like the
book is
liketheroseislikethebookisliketheroseisthecoloroftherose

CAÑON

The passage is filled with sentences.
The passage is filled with sentences.
Boulders high on the lee side of the east slope.
Boulder high on the windward side of the west slope.
The trail wends through it, tight and uneven.
The trail wends to a dead end, uneven and tight.
There is no house no structure, no question, no answer.
There is no house no question no planks no structure.
The walls are no no no no no slick no hand holds.
The walls are no no nononono sheer no hand holds.
The sky is blue the tree making it blue.
The sky is blue the green trees made blue by sky blue.
Some things reflect and some things do not.
The passage is filled with sentences.
The same better full of passages and the sentence.

Indian Yellow

at stake here
something other than a quest
repetition and reflexivity
a breakdown in meditation
affirmation discourse
a narrow logical sense
grounds reasons
conditions of possibility
neither beginning
nor a beginning
yes a nonspecular relation
affirmed self-mirrored

The selfsame is a walk through nonidentity,
a walk through nonreflexive and expansive release.

The child laid out.

So many ways to save the baby.

So many ways.

INSTATED

Doubting doubts that doubted
doubtless doubting doubts
is how we got here in the first place.

I've been lost many times and it always looks just like this.

Except for that tree. It wasn't there.

MUSE

the champagne
hardly mended the situation,
the locus,
but the coolness against
the throat,
that was especially
needed,
coolness cool cold,
more than the roaring
applause.
the voices did
little to address
the raging thirst
and drinking, as
always, was mere folly,
coolness.
he told her to meet
meet him on Pont Neuf,
never expecting
that she would show
and in fact
she did not,
but later
he would find her
near the medical school,
on the steps of the Odeon,
cold,

all beautiful,
all herself,
symmetrical,
all too much,
and he would be
crushed by
it all,
especially, if not
solely, by the fact,
solely,
that she did not
recall him,
especially his name.

ARGUMENT

we will denote by the

symbol

the proposition   always

the proposition which asserts all

the values

this proposition involves the function

not merely

an ambiguous value

of

the function

the assertion of

where   is

unspecified   is

a different assertion   the latter is

in no sense

ambiguous

KEY WEST 1975

for David Sims

Evidently,
too many
unexplained dicta burden
one's memory,
frustrate one's
judgment.
When a rubric works
and there is no
cogent, adequate elucidation,
but only a stony,
scabrous justification
chaperoned by an
agreeable notation,
script, signs,
an unclouded set of rules
serves nearly as well.
At least
for a time.
So, she told me when left.
Truman Avenue
was still dirt.

THE SCOPE OF DESCRIPTION

And so we must be able
by our own notation
to distinguish whether
the whole or only part
of our proposition is to be
treated as our definition.

Follow the dots
until we reach an equal
number of dots not
signifying a product
(shall we call it logical),
or the end of a sentence,
or a closing bracket.

will mean
but
will mean

will mean
and
will mean

And I must be able
by my own notation
to will the meaning
to some conditional
end, some product,
some closing bracket.

This Cadaverous Topography

The strangest of our rivers races muddy,
Juniper berries falling and rolling off hillsides,
Collecting notions of what is need,
Of what is want, sweeping them into
The flow, with the malm and dull roots.
The sun is forgetful and so shines again,
Surprised to find herself in her own light
And cutthroats splash in the eddies,
Along undercut banks, near some confluence.
We follow it down to a place that matters,
Where we drink coffee and remember our boots.

The strangest of our rivers divides us,
Wedges deep with the push of storms
And drives hard the harsh rush
Of events that shape our fear of each
Other.

The moon took us and showed us the springs,
Gently suggested that we not drown.
Said so with a handful of desiccated earth,
The chrome yellow reflection of his eyes in the pool.
And so the moment tells us that
Death, disillusionment, xenophobia, stupidity
Has undone so many,
What I tell you three times is true.
What I tell you three times is true.
What I tell you three times is true.

THE WEAK

There is some skein of loose dreams,
silken and unraveled against a backdrop of
                              more dreams,
and more dreams and more dreams,
and I am dying piecemeal;
                              at least I am told.

Rinsed by rain and riddled
with the icy cold of, yes, dreams,
the weak, like me, pause.

In me is the end of logic.
my wandering is sad and excessive.
The weak, like me, will call out
into a shaky wilderness
                              where cool breezes are danger.

SPECCHI

There was a boy with a twisted arm,
A twisted arm, a twisted arm had
This boy with a twisted arm and
The arm made a noise, a noise,
A pop when he moved his twisted arm,
The boy with that twisted arm.

And you couldn't tell that it was twisted,
Except that it looked twisted, his arm
Twisted like that, popping like that
When he moved it all twisted like that
That boy with that twisted arm,
The boy with that twisted arm.

But my arm is not twisted, though
It has been twisted and it even pops
At times when I move it and I move it a lot,
My arm that is not twisted, like the boy's,
That boy with the twisted arm,
A pop when he moved that twisted arm.

Misstep

Will essence play a regulative role in this dialectic.
On Archon's veranda, a king's morning?

Prosecute. Prosecute. The light of simple charge.
But what kind of charge? Tapping at the edge of holiness.

Prosecuting murder on behalf of a murderer, no
Business of the City's, but death on the wing, in the wings.

Euthyphro aims at the bushes, sling, spear in hand;
Still, he wings the beater with imagined true sight.

What is holy is what I do and I do it because
To fail to do so would be, must be, will be unholy.

But is that all that is holy? Socrates bites a cracker.
What else is holy? What else, what else and why?

What do these holy things have in common? Necessary
And sufficient to warrant this *useful* label?

Question and question, answer after answer,
Misstep and misses step, falling forward and still, still holy.

A Novel

We had no ordinary meeting.
We were no less than two strangers.
And no fewer.

THE FIRES WE SET

The world's ugliest wind
hissed along the weather-eaten slope
of dry sage with no homes.
But those who lived there,
how their spirits soared
and not in just one direction.

The sun could have been a melon
with no rind, but it was not,
but instead a slow piece of flesh
burning itself up like sadness.
Men and women worked in
that wind, without jobs, but
only work, cutting brush thicker
than the ankles of old women,
moving up slope and down,
across grain and back, cutting
like that wind against the heat,
hissing with that wind against
whatever song two towhees might
offer up in the afternoon.

There was cerulean between the quaking
leaves of the aspens.

Truth

1

Am I, will I be, structurally
imorphic,
with some state
of affairs
        hovering?
Will that
make me true?
Must the
components
of my
        self
        line
        up
like points on
a grid.
Parallel to the
truth of me,
between that truth,
and some state of affairs
that is the
        expression of a statement.

But it is all
merely idea anyway,
isn't it?
Even without a
mind. This world may
not claim its facts.

2

Truth is a property,
not property, of
a system, ascribed,
as it were,
to individual propositions,
but only
derivatively   according
with the whole.
Truth requires fit.
Will coherence and
consistency,
not the logical cousins I desire,
be sufficient to some truth?
But where shall I place
this negation?
Are all beliefs possible?
Of course they are.
Alternate geometries,
axiomatic independence.

3

What is the brand
of your reality?
It is static,
subject,
if not dependent on some
human's cognition—
independent?
Reality is in here—tap, tap.
Physical, sexual,
biological, racial—
what brand is yours?
Heraclitus set the table,
all flowing, nothing stands
still, Piaget thought Fleck
was such a Wiener.
Ontologically speaking,
verification is a pipe
dream anyway.
Reality is what it is what it is.
Meaning?
That's our job.

THE LAST CANVAS

If and when
The paint remains wet
Longer than the notion remains
Stretched like the canvas and
Fresh, I will put down my knife.
Working wet scares the spiders,
Leans tree into shadow,
Folds fair winds into troubled
Seas full of greens and blues
And the reds that are there
But unseen like the yellows.
The knife still glistens
With the Indian yellow, translucent
And rich gold light, under
The layers on layers on
Layers of bad dreams
And good dreams, bad
Intentions and found peace,
A little sleep and a nightmare
Here and there.
How many many eyes we
Meet squinting above moving
Lips, shifting alliances, odd
Motives, but the eyes are enough,
Aren't they?
Aren't they?

Rowing Through Blood

Our hands are not hands our
hands are empty and reaching
our hands and full of nothing
matters in our hands and things
are out of them.

It is ugly sad useless as
are we like a straining simile
this war this comedy this
excuse is so us unbelievably us
so embarrassingly us.

I'm told that History can be a willing
teacher to students with
a blank leaf to spare to cover
with a considered note a nod
to the quagmire of another.

It is ugly sad useless as
are we like a straining simile
this war this comedy this
excuse is so us unbelievably us
so embarrassingly us.

Our hands are not hands our
hands are empty and reaching
our hands and full of nothing
matters in our hands and things
are out of them.

Hedge

He leaves the room as if
nothing has happened,

no nods, no sidelong glances at the clock. He
leaves the grounds soft and muddy,

a crop of eyebrows, a gaggle of gagging
and gagged. Some red skies

in the morning, some foul breeze, but still
a normal stride toward the open gate,

some nerve, some daring, but none daring
to light a candle in the pitch

or to look on while the sun burns like
a sun, the truth moves like a dog on fresh

trail, like a dog, like a dog, tail-wag-gagging
into the diced, sun-starved language of history.

CONFLUENCE

With all this going on around us,
we need, we need . . . who am I to say
what we need? I need a   canyon and a river
with rocks the size of trucks,
              clouds that form in thunderheads
and kiss the very air with their approach,
hawks that promise to be anything but red tails,
the tracks of   elk in a muddy bank,
a muddy bank and a gravelly beach,
some royal coachmen tied the night before,
music that hardly anyone recalls,
books that may have all their pages,
phases of a moon that my father watched,

        a lightning strike on a meadow.

CANTER COUNTER CANTER

Can't keep the reins, hold the reins, die.
Can't keep the reins, hold the reins, die.
Pull the reins, tug the reins, pull,
See-saw, pull, tug the reins, yaw.
Feel the reins, forgive the reins,
Hold the reins, die.

Bark Bark at the Sea in November

At night the wind the red the sound
bash
against rocks and all else.

At night the sea lions bark their way
into dreams.
Fog and crash and lips and hands and

rains come and go and
fog rolls and wind waits and lions
bark and bark and bark.

At light the wind rides the light
against rocks, against itself,
into dreams, bark, bark,
bark.

NO CHANGE IN THE RED OF THE BLUE NIGHT

There is no edge.
Before, there was only a pretense of edge.
Now, there is no pretense.
Before, there was much talk
Of the edge and the system
And the movement and
The cause and conjunction
And conjunction and conjunction,
But they were only ands.
Pop music has always been
Only pop music popping along
Popped, pooped, peeped through
Little speakers by little speakers
And but that's okay, isn't it?
There is no edge,
No place to fear. No
Fear is a good thing.
Before, there was only a pretense of edge.
Sometimes bad things
Happen to bad people.
Dull things always
Happen to dull people.
Dull people always
Happen to bad things.

THE LAST TIME I SAW THIS RIVER

The last time I saw this river
                  it was wet.
There was a beaver dam over there
And the moon belonged to this canyon.
Only a few pines had browned to beetles,
A herd of elk made the air musky.

I still smoked cigars then, but that night
I didn't even burn a fire.
                I left no sign
And I'm please to say that this river
Does not remember me.

Beautiful Equations

for Miles

are out there somewhere,
calling, singing, passing candles
to the last one in line.

The shape of the moon is
different every night, the
sun grows dimmer by the hour.

It is symmetry
that makes an equation
beautiful.

Draw a line through
any point in your circle.

You can always find symmetry,

Symmetry will not, not always, not ever, find you.

PROPOSITION

Turn me around
Loop de loop
Turn me around
Loop de yea
Dance with me tomorrow

Swing me about
Hobblede bim
Swing me about
Hobblede bee
Dance with me tomorrow.

Toss me a line
Bubbly be dee
Toss me a line
Bubbly be quay
Drown with me today

If you dance with me tomorrow
If you dance with me tomorrow
If you dance with me tomorrow
I will drown with you today

SLEEPING SLEEPING

A man came upon a sleeping man
He said what is it that you makes you sleep?
The sleeping man just slept, his snoring,

A drone against the noiseless sky.
Why again the man asked whatever
Makes you sleep like that, here like that?

And the sleeping man said nothing,
But slept harder and in a different direction,
His snoring a screen with shadows behind

And then the man who had come upon him
Said nothing, but touched the sleeping man
His shoulder, his hand, his wide open eyes

And the sleeping man sat up in his
Sleeping state and slept on like a
Sleeping sleepy dead to the world man,

A sleeping man with no sun in the morning,
A sleeping man with no waves from the ocean,
A sleeping man with no hands or fingers,

A sleeping man with no legs or songs,
Just deep breathing into the dark
Deep damp world of dead dead sleep.

THE MONKEYS

If there is a light on that mountain,
That high place surrounded by low,
It is fire, perhaps pushed by some wind,
Or some friction of winds,
Perhaps consuming all that is in one spot.
If there is a light on that mountain,
It is a reflection, perhaps of something,
Perhaps a reflection of a reflection
Of the fire of the man that lives up
Thirteen-Mile road making experiments
With chemicals and monkeys
That run out into the road at night
On that mountain where there is
A light on that mountain.

THE RAIN

for Danzy

The rain was wet and falling
so wet and falling down
wet and from the up it fell
the rain was wet and falling

the rain fell through the sun
the rain fell through the clouds
wet from head to tail
the rain was wet and falling

the rain fell blue and silver
from left to right and down
wet from morning to somewhere past noon
the rain was wet and falling

the rain smelled of zinc and blood
it made a sound like hawks
the rain spoke one syllable at a time
the rain was wet and falling

CONDITIONS

It is as if and when the if
Was then and when it was and if
And when then it came to if
When only it was if and when as
When it was less than then
As where whereas if then

All conditionals then are such
Only if the if then is where the if
Is then where the then and not the if
Was where the if and not the
Then was where it was

If and only if and iffy whiffy
Then about where the whiffy iffy
Is and where the then falls about
The if and if the only if is where
The if and only if is found.

FIRE

The moon sings down
                    the echoes,
the echoes close out the voices,
the night
is lined with silk and intentions,
good and bad,   echoes and
and rain fall somewhere up canyon
while a man who might be
a father stands in front of a
fire in a great room, pointing
to the alder logs,
speaking to some logic   echoes
good or bad, and
rain falls without notice
somewhere,   echoes
perhaps up canyon,
while a man who
might be a son pretends to
pretend that he is pretending
that echoes repeat and
echoes fall
          and echoes ring
like all the echoes before
and to come
and to come
and to come.

KINDER

for Miles and Henry

They are small now,
negotiating the business of sharing.
snatching is a part of it, crying is much of it, power is
all of it and crawling comes
slow to the younger one,

going slow comes slow to the older.
they talk about their Papa when he is away, want
their mommy when he is present,
fixing toys, like

his job description says,
like his heart tells him to. He will fix it
all for a hug, break it all
and fix it again, fix it again, fix it again

for a laugh, for the sound of *Papa Papa*.
His sons own him. He is their property.
Coins in their pockets,
cars in their box,
paper in their books
waiting for lines, for colors.

SLOWLY DARK COMES

I sit by the fire we have built
Touching each spike of flame, watching
Light slide along the wall.
I ask for nothing in this silence,
In this endless dusk,
As dark drags its heels home.

A moon sits up straight,
Shaped so strange and unlike last night's.
Who would count the craters
To find the same nakedness,
To find the same light.
Broken music is the moon's.

Come closer, come closer,
The dark will be here soon enough.
We will huddle like in a warren,
Keeping warm against the promise
Of the darkness, the night
And the light to follow.

OF MINIMAL THINGS

each slope veers itself to the other,
being always already on the opposite slope,

the sole condition of hope and truth,
words already insidiously causing passage

from one slope to the other, changing you
into something that you were not before.

MAPS

Photos betrayed me as I wandered
Sing a song long into the night

Into the landscapes I would love,
Sing a song for me into the night

As I walked sideways into the canyons
Singing song into the night

That had already been rendered
Sing a song into the night

But·you came to me like the arches
Sing our song into this night

Curved in the space of my being, framing
Songs sung singing into the night

A view west or east, stopping no light,
Stopping no wind, but

Singing songs into the night,
The night singing back into the night.

GIFT

the world is fish and water,
water and fish, and a dream of fish
fishing for fish in the water where fish fish

and if you love love as deep as
fish will fish then love will love you,
love, deeply, as love loves

give and take the giving for the
last take, the given take and give and take
and all the taking takes the given

BIOGRAPHICAL NOTE

Percival Everett is the author of sixteen novels, three collections of short fiction, and two volumes of poetry. He is the recipient of the PEN Center USA Award for Fiction, the Academy Award from the American Academy of Arts and Letters, the Hurston/Wright Legacy Award, the PEN/Oakland-Josephine Miles Award for Excellence in Literature, and a New American Writing Award. His stories have been included in the *Pushcart Prize Anthology* and *Best American Short Stories*. He has served as a judge for, among others, the 1997 National Book Award for fiction and the PEN/Faulkner Award for Fiction in 1991. He teaches fiction writing and critical theory and is currently Distinguished Professor of English at the University of Southern California in Los Angeles.